AI+ME

Big Idea #4

Intelligent agents require many kinds of knowledge to interact naturally with humans.

People interact with each other using different ways.

Most people can talk to other people.

Besides talking, people also write, use body language, change their tone of voice, and use their hands to interact with other people.

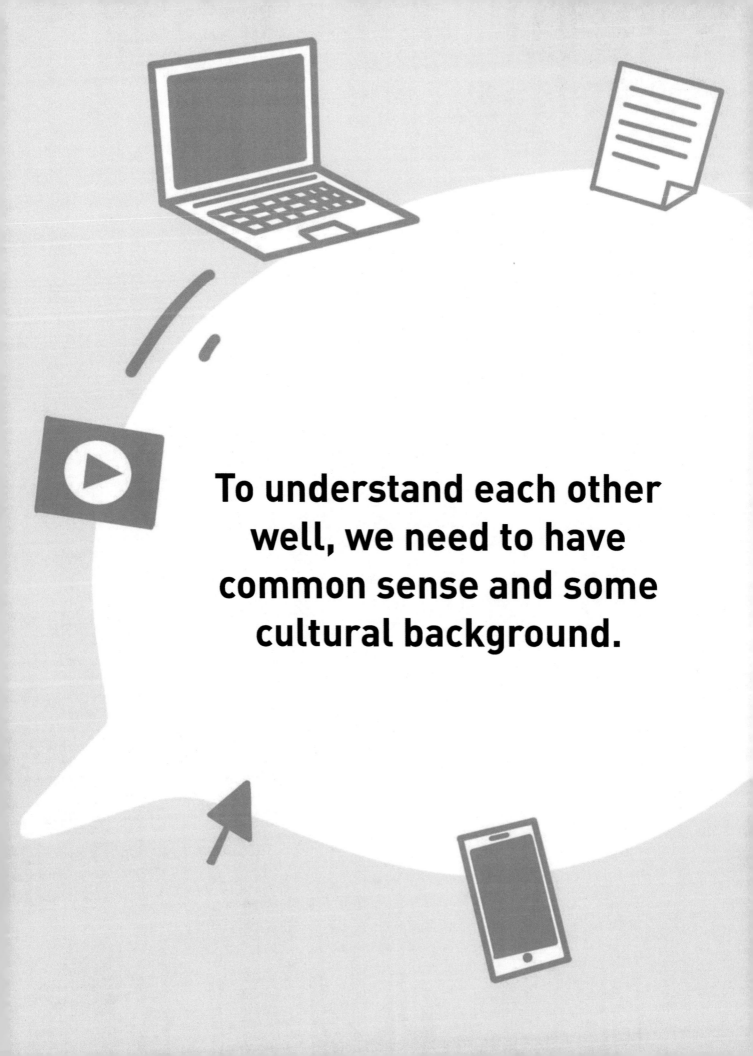

To understand each other well, we need to have common sense and some cultural background.

Let's explore some of the knowledge AI needs in order to understand human language and talk to us.

Can computers speak?

Sure! Computers can be programmed to speak. This is called speech generation.

But interacting is more than speaking. Interacting needs a back and forth.

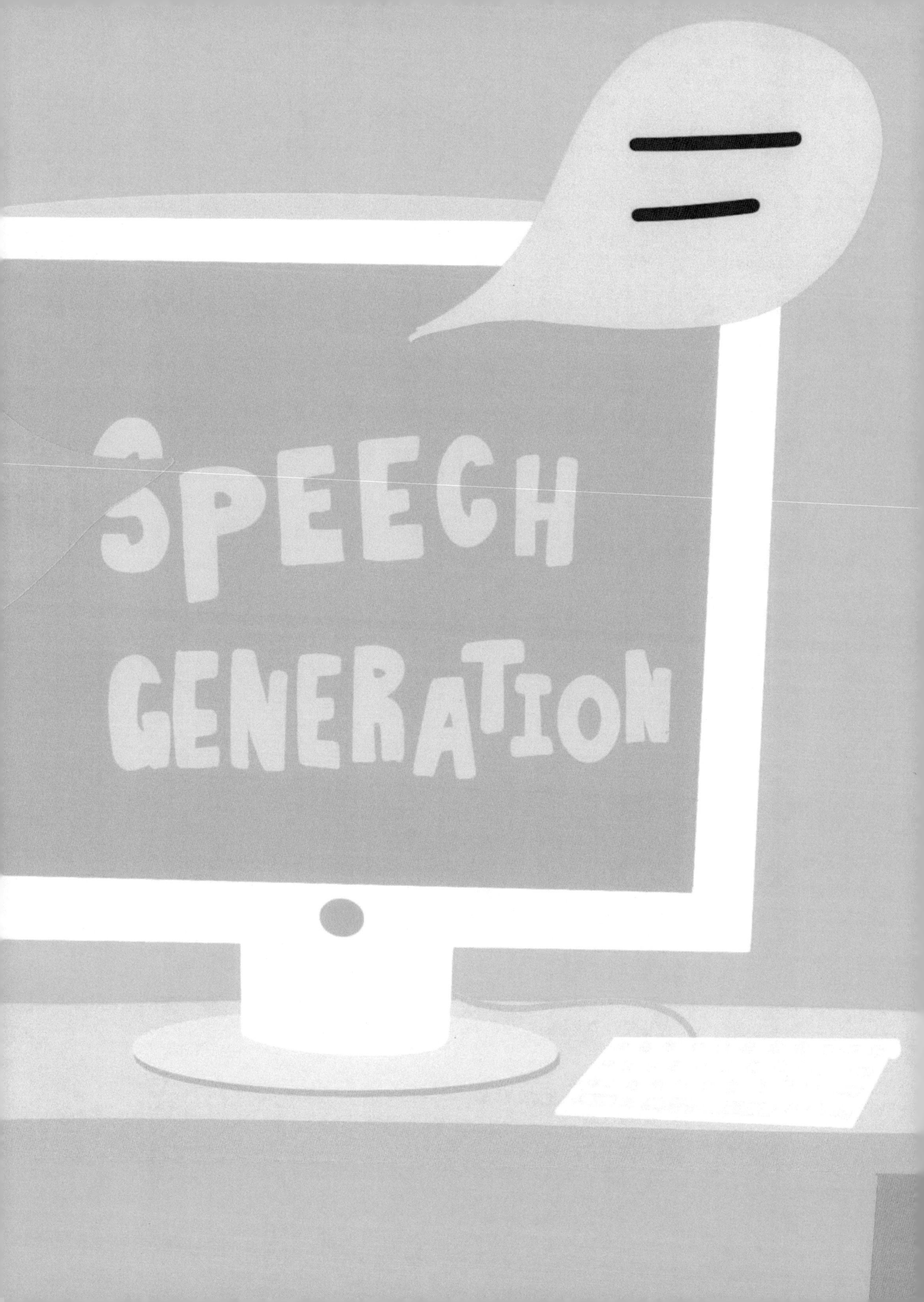
SPEECH
GENERATION

Can computers hear us?

Sure! AI can understand spoken language. This is called speech recognition.

But AI needs knowledge in order to understand what we mean.

SPEECH RECOGNITION

Digital assistants like Siri and Alexa can listen and respond in human languages.

But it's hard to talk to Siri or Alexa for very long. They don't remember things you said earlier. And they don't share the same common sense as you have.

It's partly cloudy, with a high of 72°F.

What would AI need to have a real conversation with us?

Imagine a British English speaker interacting with a computer taught by American English speakers.

They both speak English. But their English is different. AI needs the knowledge of different cultures to help it decide the meaning of sentences.

One sentence could mean different things depending on the context.

Here is another example.

"The chicken is ready to eat."

Here are some other examples with words that have more than one meaning.

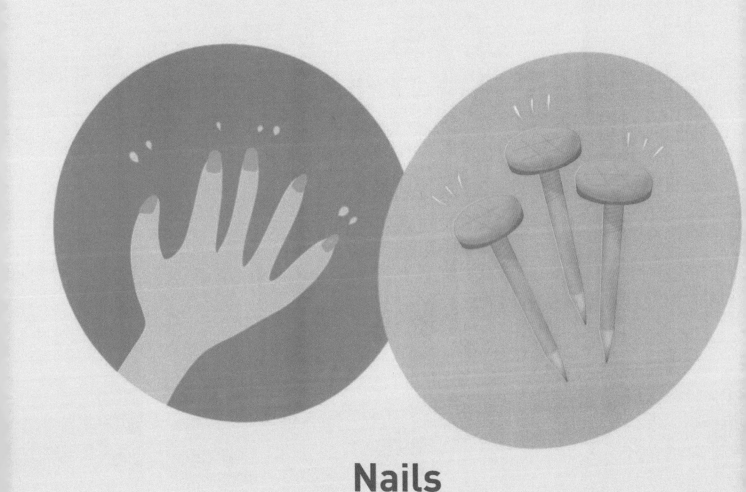

Nails

Understanding context could help AI understand what we mean.

Bark

Meaning can also change based on tone and body language.

Which person really means "Good job"?

Good job!

AI can't understand your tone. It doesn't know if you are happy, angry, sad, or excited.

Look at the image.
What should AI give to the girl?

Give me the mouse, please!

Use your common knowledge to help AI.

This is a problem that Alan Turing, a pioneer in AI, thought a lot about. He asked,

"Could a machine ever be intelligent?"

He said that the answer would be "yes" if the machine could hold an intelligent conversation.

Alan Turing invented a test that we now call the Turing Test.

Imagine a person is having a conversation via text with two individuals. One is a human and the other is a computer.

The Turing Test says that a computer can be called intelligent if it can fool a human into thinking that it was a person.

No AI system built so far can pass the Turing Test.

But some chatbots are trained to have simple conversations with people on specific topics.

When you are shopping online, a chatbot can answer almost all of your questions about products.

Where is my package?

What's your tracking number?

Many scientists are working on something called "Natural Language Processing," which means computers can understand and use language the way people do. Some of them have made great progress.

For example, Google does a good job translating passages of text into different languages.

Still, AI has a long way to go to interact naturally with humans.

Maybe you'll help teach AI to interact more naturally with us, and we'll be able to talk with an AI the same way we talk with our friends.

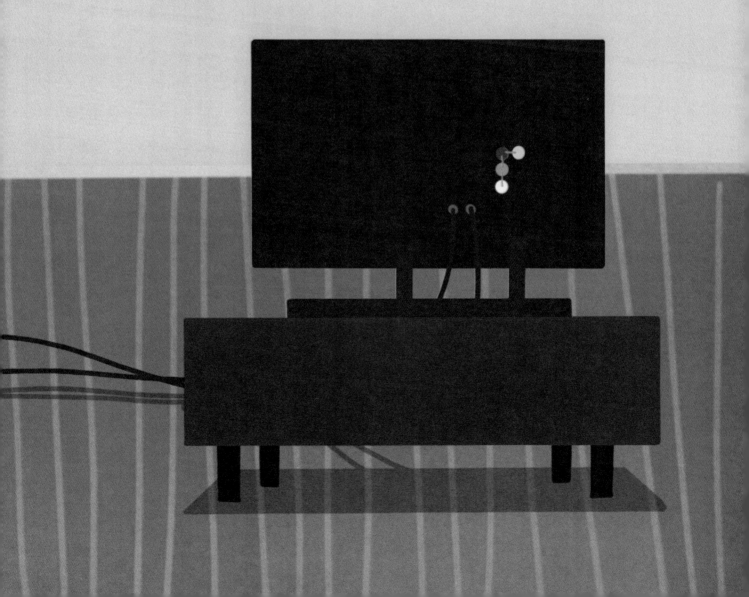

How would you test a computer to see if it is *really* intelligent?

AI+Me

BIG IDEA #4
HUMAN-AI INTERACTION

Go to edu.readyai.org to get your online certificate and badge now!

More AI+Me badges await you!

BIG IDEA #1
PERCEPTION

BIG IDEA #2
REPRESENTATION & REASONING

BIG IDEA #3
MACHINE LEARNING

BIG IDEA #5
SOCIETAL IMPACT

"AI+ME" is a free online experience intended to provide young learners with the basics of AI. The lesson takes about one hour to complete.

You can earn badges for all Five Big Ideas if you finish all topics with full score and visit the summary page at the end of each slide.

Dear Reader,

I hope you enjoyed reading about the challenges of getting computers to communicate naturally with people. Our lives will be enriched by interacting with intellgient agents that can understand our thinking and sense our moods, even if they can not yet pass the Turing test. Humans are among the hardest things for computers to emulate, because we are so wonderfully complex. But as AI continues to advance, our computers will become even better companions.

Dr. David S. Touretzky
Professor of Computer Science, Carnegie Mellon University
Founder, AI4K12 Initiative
Member of the Advisory Board, ReadyAI

Five Big Ideas in AI

Perception (Big Idea #1): Computers perceive the world using sensors.

Representation & Reasoning (Big Idea #2): Agents maintain models/ representations of the world and use them for reasoning.

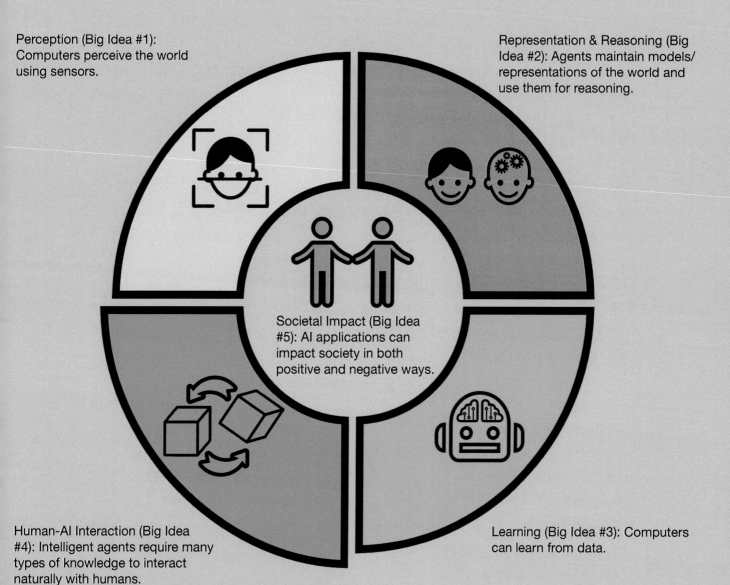

Societal Impact (Big Idea #5): AI applications can impact society in both positive and negative ways.

Human-AI Interaction (Big Idea #4): Intelligent agents require many types of knowledge to interact naturally with humans.

Learning (Big Idea #3): Computers can learn from data.

"Five Big Ideas in AI" are K-12 AI guidelines designed by AI4K12, a joint initiative of AAAI (the Association for the Advancement of Artificial Intelligence) and CSTA (the Computer Science Teachers Association)

Dear Parents,

Many grown-ups view self-driving cars, Siri, Alexa voice assistance, and other considered cool artificial intelligence (AI) technologies as revolutionary, radical, and, at times, even annoying. Our kids don't share our views. To them, AI makes perfect sense. Look at how kids ask their Alexa device questions that we, as adults, would not. In the next decade or so for most kids, AI will be their co-workers, drivers, insurance agents, customer service representatives, bank tellers, receptionists, radiologists, in short, a natural part of their lives.

As grown-ups, we have an important responsibility to prepare our children so they can use AI effectively, understand the inherent limitations, and build a better future using the technology.

Our core belief at ReadyAI is that children around the world should have the right to be AI-educated so they can thrive intellectually and emotionally alongside AI. Investing in every child can transform them from passive spectators of technology disruption to active participants of positive change in their local communities and the world at large.

Artificial intelligence will soon play a role in decisions that are much more important than the movies we watch on Netflix, the music we play on Spotify, or the news stories Facebook recommends us. We owe it to our children not only to help them understand and utilize the powerful tools of AI but also to thoughtfully weigh its moral and social implications early on.

We can do this together.

Roozbeh Aliabadi
CEO, ReadyAI

AI+Me Series

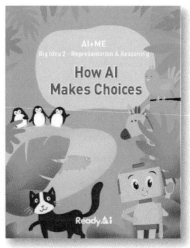

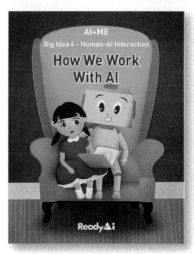

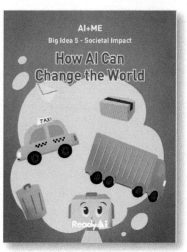

Artist & Designer:
Shanshan Jin

Consultants:
Dr. David S. Touretzky
Joel Wilson

ReadyAi

Made in the USA
Las Vegas, NV
30 May 2023

72717238R00026